GUIDING IN THE DUST

A LEADER'S COMPANION TO DUSTPRINTS OF THE RABBI

A COVENANT PATH™ SERIES LEADER GUIDE
BOOK 1.2

RICH VAN DOORN

To every leader who said yes—
even when you felt unworthy, uncertain, or unprepared.
Your obedience matters more than your confidence.
Thank you for guiding others in the Rabbi's dust.

*And to **Max Andrews**—*
your quiet strength, faithful presence, and servant leadership
helped shape the kind of guide I hope to become.
Thank you for walking ahead with grace.

FOREWORD

If you're holding this guide, there's a good chance you've been asked to lead others down a path you're still walking yourself. Maybe you feel the weight of that. Maybe you're battling a quiet voice whispering, *"Who am I to lead anyone?"* I know that voice. I've heard it too.

You're not alone.

Leadership in the Kingdom has never been about perfection. It's not about having all the answers or mastering every concept. In fact, the best leaders are often the ones still limping from the journey—still learning, still wrestling, still clinging to the dust-covered feet of the Rabbi.

Guiding in the Dust isn't a manual of expertise. It's a companion—designed to walk with you as you help others follow Jesus more closely. It pairs with *Dustprints of the Rabbi* and the companion devotional *Walking in the Dust* to create a layered experience of study, reflection, and shared transformation.

This guide offers structure and insight, but it doesn't replace the Spirit. It gives cultural context, but it won't replace your authenticity. What your group needs most isn't a polished expert—it's a present disciple. Someone willing to go first. To ask the hard questions. To admit the struggle. To keep showing up.

That's you.

So if you're feeling unqualified, take heart. The Rabbi has always chosen ordinary people to do extraordinary things. Not because they had it all together—but because they were willing to walk behind Him, even when the path was dusty and hard.

May this guide serve your calling well.

And may you discover, week by week, that His strength really is made perfect in our weakness.

> *Lead from the dust.*
> *Lead with grace.*
> *And never stop following.*

—Rich Van Doorn

THE COVENANT PATH™
SERIES MAP

WALKING THE WAY OF THE RABBI — ONE
BOOK, ONE STEP AT A TIME

Your Journey Has Begun...

This Leader Guide — *Guiding in the Dust* — is the next step in a 17-book discipleship journey.

Each book in *The Covenant Path* ™ series is paired with:

- A **Core Book** – Theological and historical foundations
- A **Devotional** – Six-day spiritual practice + Sabbath reflection
- A **Leader Guide** – Cultural insights, Hebraic terms, and small group support

THE COVENANT PATH™ SERIES (CONFIRMED TITLES & SUBTITLES)

1. **Dustprints of the Rabbi**: *Discipleship in the Texture of Torah and Grace*

HOW TO KEEP WALKING

Each step includes:

- A teaching book
- A companion devotional
- A leader guide like this one

Start with the next title — or gather a new group to walk through this one again.

Discipleship is not a class. It's a path. The Rabbi is still walking. So must we.

INTRODUCTION – WELCOME TO THE DUST

DUSTPRINTS OF THE RABBI — THE COVENANT PATH™ LEADER SERIES

"Let your house be a meeting place for the wise; sit in the dust of their feet and drink in their words with thirst."

— *PIRKEI AVOT 1:4*

WHY THIS GUIDE EXISTS

Discipleship is more than belief — it's a way of life. *Dustprints of the Rabbi* invites readers to walk behind Jesus, the first-century Jewish Rabbi who still calls followers today. But few journeys are meant to be walked alone. That's where you come in.

Guiding in the Dust is your companion as you lead others through this transformational path. Whether you're meeting in a living room, after church, in a classroom, or around a coffee table, this guide helps you create sacred space for reflection, conversation, and action.

You don't need to be a theologian — you just need to be a little dusty.

WHAT YOU'RE LEADING

Each of the 14 sessions in this guide corresponds to the chapters in *Dustprints of the Rabbi* and the weekly devotional, *Walking in the Dust*. These three resources form one integrated journey:

- **The Book** (Dustprints of the Rabbi): Core teaching and theological depth
- **The Devotional** (Walking in the Dust): Daily Scripture, reflection, and practice
- **This Guide** (Guiding in the Dust): Weekly group facilitation, insights, and support

---

WHAT YOU'LL FIND EACH WEEK

Each session follows a consistent structure to keep things simple and flexible:

1. **Session Overview** — Title, focus verse, theme, and weekly leader objective
2. **Opening Prayer & Shema** — A moment to settle and center
3. **Grounding in the Dust** — Hebraic or cultural insight, with term definitions
4. **Recap & Reflection** — Book and devotional highlights

5. **Group Discussion** — Curated questions to spark dialogue
6. **Dustprint Discipleship Challenge** — A call to real-life practice
7. **Closing Prayer & Blessing** — A shared moment to seal the session

---

A NOTE ON HEBRAIC TERMS

You'll encounter words like *Talmid* (disciple), *Halakhah* (way of walking), *Midrash* (interpretive commentary), and others rooted in the Jewish worldview of Jesus. Each is briefly explained within the session to give you confidence and clarity as you lead.

YOU DON'T HAVE TO KNOW IT ALL

Remember, the goal is not to have every answer. Your goal is to host the dust — to create an environment where people can walk more closely behind the Rabbi. Be present. Be curious. Be faithful.

Jesus does the forming. You simply hold the space.

LEADER COVENANT &
COMMITMENT

WALKING IN THE DUST TOGETHER

"Whoever wants to be great among you must be your servant."

— MATTHEW 20:26

As a leader on The Covenant Path™, I commit to:

1. Walk Behind the Rabbi First
I will lead not from arrival, but from pursuit. I will walk behind Jesus — not just talk about Him. My leadership will flow from discipleship.

2. Create Space for Formation
I will foster environments where others can wrestle, wonder, listen, and grow. I will lead with grace, humility, and spiritual curiosity.

3. Honor the Hebraic Roots of Our Faith

I will approach this journey with reverence for the Jewish worldview of Jesus and the first-century context of His teaching. I will define terms, invite questions, and point others to the richness of Scripture in its original setting.

4. Uphold Unity and Confidentiality

I will protect the sacred space of group conversations. What is shared in the group stays in the group, unless there is a need for loving accountability or safety.

5. Practice What I Facilitate

I will not call others to a path I am unwilling to walk myself. I will engage the devotional, reflect on the book, and live out the truth I ask others to explore.

6. Pray Before I Plan
I will lead prayerfully, not just practically. I will ask the Spirit of the Rabbi to guide each session and each heart — including mine.

LEADER COVENANT AFFIRMATION

Name: _______________________________________

Date: _______________________________________

"Rabbi Jesus, I offer You my steps, my words, my silence, and my leadership. May I guide others only as I follow You. Let my feet stay in the dust, and let those who follow me find You there. Amen."

HOW TO USE THIS GUIDE

A SIMPLE ROADMAP FOR LEADERS ON THE COVENANT PATH™

WHAT THIS GUIDE IS FOR

Guiding in the Dust is designed to help you lead others through **Dustprints of the Rabbi** — not just by reading, but by *living* it. Whether you're gathering in a home, church, café, or mentoring relationship, this guide provides the structure and depth you need to walk your group through a 14-week journey of spiritual formation.

You don't need to be an expert. You simply need to be someone walking behind the Rabbi — and inviting others to walk with you.

Each week matches one chapter from the **Book** (*Dustprints of the Rabbi*) and one week from the **Devotional** (*Walking in the Dust*). These three tools work together:

- **The Book** – Gives the historical, theological, and covenantal foundation.
- **The Devotional** – Offers six days of Scripture, reflection, and practice.
- **This Leader Guide** – Helps you create space for discussion, prayer, insight, and action.

WHAT TO EXPECT EACH WEEK

Each of the 14 sessions in this guide includes:

1. **Session Overview**
   - Title, focus verse, weekly theme, and a clear objective for the session
2. **Opening Prayer & Shema**
   - A moment to begin with Scripture and intentionality
3. **Grounding in the Dust**
   - Hebraic/cultural insight with defined terms to root the theme in context
4. **Recap & Reflection**
   - A quick summary of the book/devotional theme to center the discussion
5. **Group Discussion**
   - Curated questions to guide conversation, observation, and application
6. **Dustprint Discipleship Challenge**

  - ◦ A simple, focused way to live out the session in the coming week
7. **Closing Prayer & Blessing**
  - ◦ To end with unity, vision, and peace

WHAT IF I DON'T HAVE THE ANSWERS?

Perfect. That makes you a disciple.

Your goal is not to give a lecture — it's to *host the dust* and hold the space where Jesus can form people through Scripture, context, and community. Listen more than you talk. Pray more than you plan. And trust that the Rabbi is doing the deeper work.

SESSION 1 – DUST ON YOUR FEET

ALIGNED WITH CHAPTER 1 OF DUSTPRINTS OF THE RABBI & WEEK 1 OF WALKING IN THE DUST

Focus Verse

"Follow Me."

— MATTHEW 4:19

Theme: Discipleship begins not with understanding, but with movement. The first step is always proximity — walking close enough behind the Rabbi for His dust to mark your life.

Leader Objective: By the end of this session, group members will be able to describe the first-century meaning of "following a rabbi," reflect on their own response to Jesus' call, and identify where they need to trust Him enough to take the next step.

1. OPENING PRAYER & SHEMA

Open with a short prayer from the heart or use this prompt:

Prayer Prompt:
Jesus, we don't want to just learn about You — we want to follow You. Even when we don't understand where You're going. Let Your dust cling to us today.
Amen.

Optional Shema (Deuteronomy 6:4–5):
"Hear, O Israel: The LORD our God, the LORD is one.
Love the LORD your God with all your heart and with all your soul and with all your strength."

---

2. GROUNDING IN THE DUST (CULTURAL INSIGHT)

In the first century, rabbis didn't invite students to classrooms. They invited them to **walk** — literally. To be a disciple (*talmid*) meant to follow your rabbi so closely that the dust from his feet would cover yours.

Mishnah Insight:

"Let your house be a meeting place for sages; sit in the dust of their feet and drink in their words with thirst."

— PIRKEI AVOT 1:4

This was the model of a **talmid (תלמיד)** — a disciple who not only learned his teacher's words, but studied his way of life. The plural form is **talmidim (תלמידים)**. These disciples aimed to follow so closely that their rabbi's dust would cling to their clothes.

Following a rabbi also meant submitting to his **ol (עוֹל)** — his "yoke." This was not a burden but a symbol of voluntary alignment to the rabbi's **halakhah (הֲלָכָה)** — his interpretation of how to live out the Torah. To take on the rabbi's yoke was to adopt his lifestyle, priorities, and convictions.

Hebraic Terms Introduced This Week:

- **Talmid / Talmidim** – Disciple(s); one who follows a rabbi's way of life.
- **Ol** – Yoke; symbolic of submitting to a rabbi's authority and teaching.
- **Halakhah** – "The way one walks"; a rabbi's practical application of Torah.

3. RECAP & REFLECTION (BOOK + DEVOTIONAL HIGHLIGHTS)

Book Recap – Dustprints of the Rabbi (Chapter 1):
Discipleship begins in movement. Jesus called Peter without offering a five-year plan — just the invitation: *"Follow Me."* Like the first-century rabbis, Jesus expected His disciples to drop everything and walk behind Him. The dust was proof of proximity — and proximity was the point.

Devotional Tie-In – Walking in the Dust (Week 1):
Each day of the devotional this week explored what it means to follow without clarity. Whether it was Peter dropping nets, Abraham leaving his homeland, or a missionary walking without applause — the theme was consistent: trust the Rabbi enough to move.

4. GROUP DISCUSSION QUESTIONS

You don't need to use all of these. Choose 4–5 that best fit your group's time and tone.

1. *What stood out to you from the book or devotional this week?*
2. *What do you think Peter felt when Jesus simply said, "Follow Me"?*
3. *How would you describe your current proximity to Jesus — close, distant, hesitant?*
4. *What "net" (habit, identity, expectation) might Jesus be asking you to drop?*
5. *What keeps you from moving forward when the destination isn't clear?*

6. *Who has walked closely enough behind Jesus that their dust has touched your life?*

5. DUSTPRINT DISCIPLESHIP CHALLENGE

Invite your group to take one step this week that reflects obedience without clarity.

Challenge Prompt (from Devotional):
Take a visible step behind Jesus:

- Let go of a distraction.
- Take up a new rhythm.
- Pray, speak, or serve even if no one sees.

Encourage them to reflect on how it felt — and what dust it may have stirred.

6. CLOSING PRAYER & GROUP BLESSING

Prayer Prompt:
Jesus, we don't always know the road. But we want to follow You anyway. Give us courage to move, to trust, and to walk close enough for the dust to cling.
Amen.

Optional Blessing (spoken together):

"We walk in the dust of the Rabbi — and we do not walk alone."

SESSION 2 – COME AND SEE

ALIGNED WITH CHAPTER 2 OF DUSTPRINTS OF THE RABBI & WEEK 2 OF WALKING IN THE DUST

Focus Verse

"Come," He replied, "and you will see."

— JOHN 1:39

Theme: Discipleship begins with invitation and presence — not certainty. The Rabbi doesn't demand full understanding before He welcomes you near.

Leader Objective: By the end of this session, participants will understand the relational nature of Jesus' call to "Come and see," reflect on how they've responded to His invitation personally, and identify how to draw closer even amid spiritual questions or uncertainty.

1. OPENING PRAYER & SHEMA

Prayer Prompt:
Rabbi Jesus, thank You for not waiting until we have it all figured out. You simply say, "Come and see." Give us hearts to move closer, eyes to see more clearly, and trust to keep following You this week. Amen.

Optional Shema (Deuteronomy 6:4–5):
"Hear, O Israel: The LORD our God, the LORD is one.
Love the LORD your God with all your heart and with all
your soul and with all your strength."

---

2. GROUNDING IN THE DUST (CULTURAL INSIGHT)

In Jewish tradition, learning began with **presence**, not performance. To follow a **rabbi (רַבִּי)** meant first being *with* him — watching how he lived, where he dwelled, how he treated others, and how he rested.

When Jesus invited Andrew and the others to *"Come and see"*, He wasn't offering a class — He was inviting them into His life.

Mishnah Insight:
"Get yourself a teacher, acquire for yourself a companion,
and judge everyone with the scale weighted in your favor."

— PIRKEI AVOT 1:6

This form of relational discipleship expected closeness before clarity. You didn't become a **talmid (תלמיד)** — a disciple — by acing a test. You became one by saying yes to walking behind the Rabbi. This was also the beginning of one's exposure to his **halakhah (הֲלָכָה)** — his way of interpreting how the Torah is walked out in daily life.

Hebraic Terms Introduced This Week:

- **Talmid / Talmidim** – Disciple(s); one who follows a rabbi's life and teachings.
- **Halakhah** – "Way of walking"; a rabbi's personal application of Torah, embodied in life.
- **Rabbi** – Teacher, but more than an instructor — a spiritual guide, interpreter, and model.

3. RECAP & REFLECTION (BOOK + DEVOTIONAL HIGHLIGHTS)

Book Recap – Dustprints of the Rabbi (Chapter 2):
When Jesus called His first disciples, He didn't begin with explanation — He began with invitation. The first question Jesus asked wasn't "Do you believe?" but "What are you seeking?" Discipleship starts when someone draws near enough to *see* who the Rabbi really is.

Devotional Tie-In – Walking in the Dust (Week 2):
This week's devotional highlighted stories like Abraham leaving home, Moses turning aside to see the burning bush, and the disciples watching where Jesus stayed. All began with a simple posture: *availability*. Each story emphasized that God doesn't require full understanding before He reveals more — just willingness to come close.

4. GROUP DISCUSSION QUESTIONS

Choose questions that best suit your group's setting and tone:

1. *What stood out to you in the reading or devotional this week?*
2. *Why do you think Jesus said "Come and see" instead of explaining everything first?*
3. *What does it look like in today's world to respond like a talmid — even with unanswered questions?*
4. *How has your walk with Jesus involved seasons of curiosity, doubt, or discovery?*
5. *What spiritual invitation are you sensing right now — and what's holding you back from stepping toward it?*
6. *What do you need to see more clearly about Jesus in this season?*

5. DUSTPRINT DISCIPLESHIP CHALLENGE

Challenge Prompt (from Devotional):
This week, respond to the invitation to "Come and see" by practicing presence before clarity.

Encourage your group to:

- Sit in silence for five minutes daily and ask, "Jesus, where are You staying?"
- Observe where God is at work in someone else's life and thank Him.
- Invite someone to explore Jesus with you — not with answers, but with openness.

6. CLOSING PRAYER & GROUP BLESSING

Prayer Prompt:
Rabbi Jesus, Thank You for inviting us into Your presence, even when we don't have it all figured out. Help us respond like Andrew — to come and see, and to stay with You wherever You dwell. Let our closeness lead to clarity.
Amen.

Optional Group Blessing (spoken together):

"We follow the Rabbi not because we understand — but because we've seen enough to trust."

SESSION 3 – THE YOKE WE CARRY

ALIGNED WITH CHAPTER 3 OF DUSTPRINTS OF THE RABBI & WEEK 3 OF WALKING IN THE DUST

Focus Verse

"Take My yoke upon you and learn from Me, for I am gentle and humble in heart, and you will find rest for your souls."

— MATTHEW 11:29

Theme: To follow a rabbi was to take on his yoke — his teaching, his interpretation, and his way of life. Jesus offers us a yoke that doesn't demand perfection, but proximity, humility, and trust.

Leader Objective: By the end of this session, group members will understand the significance of the "yoke" in first-century discipleship, identify where they've taken on false burdens, and respond to Jesus' invitation to walk in rhythm with Him.

---

1. OPENING PRAYER & SHEMA

Prayer Prompt:
Jesus, we come tired. Some of us are carrying burdens You never gave us. Today, teach us to walk with You again — to take on Your yoke, not the world's. Let Your rhythm shape our hearts.
Amen.

Optional Shema (Deuteronomy 6:4–5):
"Hear, O Israel: The LORD our God, the LORD is one.
Love the LORD your God with all your heart and with all your soul and with all your strength."

---

2. GROUNDING IN THE DUST (CULTURAL INSIGHT)

In the first-century Jewish world, to take on a rabbi's **yoke** (*ol,* עוֹל) meant full submission to his **halakhah** — his specific interpretation of how to live out the **Torah.**

Torah (תּוֹרָה): *Literally "instruction" or "teaching." Often refers to the first five books of the Hebrew Bible (Genesis–Deuteronomy), but more broadly to God's revealed way for living.*

Halakhah (הֲלָכָה): *"The way one walks." A rabbi's halakhah included not just biblical interpretation, but modeled behavior — how to eat, rest, speak, pray, and serve. In contrast to the heavy and often legalistic yokes of some*

*Pharisees, Jesus invited His talmidim (disciples) to take on a
yoke that was **gentle and restful**, rooted in covenant love,
not performance.*

Midrash (מִדְרָשׁ): *Rabbinic storytelling and interpretive
commentary that expands and explores the layers of Scripture through creativity, questions, and imagination.*

Mishnah (מִשְׁנָה): *The first written record of Jewish oral
law (c. 200 CE). The Mishnah and Midrash formed the
framework for much of Jesus' contemporary rabbinic
discourse — and His challenge to it.*

---

3. RECAP & REFLECTION (BOOK + DEVOTIONAL HIGHLIGHTS)

Book Recap – Dustprints of the Rabbi (Chapter 3):
To take on Jesus' yoke is to align your life with His teaching,
pace, and person. While religious leaders of the day laid
heavy burdens, Jesus offered something radically different —
a yoke that is light *because it is shared*. He teaches as a Rabbi
who walks with His disciples, not ahead of them.

Devotional Tie-In – Walking in the Dust (Week 3):
This week's entries challenged readers to examine the false
yokes they carry: performance, people-pleasing, busyness, or
fear. It invited them to surrender these and take on Jesus'
halakhah — the way of mercy, humility, and rest.

4. GROUP DISCUSSION QUESTIONS

Choose 4–6 questions that best fit your group's flow:

1. *What does the idea of a "yoke" mean to you — before and after this week?*
2. *How does Jesus' yoke differ from the burdens we often carry?*
3. *What "false yokes" have you picked up that are weighing you down?*
4. *What rhythms in your life reveal your alignment — or misalignment — with the Rabbi?*
5. *How might walking in Jesus' halakhah (way of life) reframe how you work, rest, or respond to pressure?*
6. *What would it mean to truly believe His yoke is "gentle and humble in heart"?*

5. DUSTPRINT DISCIPLESHIP CHALLENGE

Challenge Prompt (from Devotional):
Take one intentional step this week to trade a false yoke for Jesus' yoke:

- Set down a pressure, habit, or expectation that doesn't reflect His gentleness.
- Ask daily: *"Jesus, am I walking in Your rhythm — or someone else's?"*
- Memorize Matthew 11:28–30 and pray it aloud each morning.

6. CLOSING PRAYER & GROUP BLESSING

Prayer Prompt:

Jesus, Some of us carry what You never asked us to bear. You offer rest, not religion. Presence, not pressure. Teach us to walk with You again — in step, in rhythm, in surrender.
Amen.

Optional Group Blessing (spoken together):

"We walk in the dust of the Rabbi — with His yoke, not our own."

SESSION 4 – HONOR AND SHAME

ALIGNED WITH CHAPTER 4 OF DUSTPRINTS OF THE RABBI & WEEK 4 OF WALKING IN THE DUST

FOCUS VERSE

"For the joy set before Him He endured the cross, scorning its shame..."

— HEBREWS 12:2

Theme: The Kingdom of God doesn't operate by the world's honor-shame standards. Jesus redefined greatness through humility, and worth through belonging — not by social status or performance.

Leader Objective: By the end of this session, group members will understand the biblical and cultural weight of honor and shame in Jesus' time, reflect on how shame affects their faith journey, and explore how the Rabbi restores dignity where the world has taken it away.

1. OPENING PRAYER & SHEMA

Prayer Prompt:
Jesus, we carry shame — sometimes silently, sometimes openly. Teach us to see ourselves the way You see us. Restore our dignity. Renew our trust. Lead us in the dust of a new kind of honor. Amen.

Optional Shema (Deuteronomy 6:4–5):
"Hear, O Israel: The LORD our God, the LORD is one.
Love the LORD your God with all your heart and with all your soul and with all your strength."

2. GROUNDING IN THE DUST (CULTURAL INSIGHT)

In Jesus' first-century Jewish context, **honor and shame** were public currencies. Status, reputation, family identity, and community acceptance defined your value. To lose honor was to risk **social exclusion**, economic loss, and religious rejection.

Mishnah Insight:
"Who is honored? He who honors others."

— AVOT 4:1

Jesus constantly disrupted this system:

- Welcoming sinners (Luke 15)
- Restoring women with public shame (Luke 7, John 8)
- Healing lepers who had been cast out (Luke 17)

He honored the dishonored and redefined belonging around Himself.

Talmud Insight:

"Great is human dignity, for it overrides a negative commandment."

— BERAKHOT 19B

Talmud (תַּלְמוּד): *The foundational collection of rabbinic discussions, laws, stories, and interpretations of the Torah, compiled after the Mishnah. It shaped Jewish thought and community life.*

Hebraic Terms Introduced This Week:

- **Talmud** – A body of rabbinic teachings that preserves the interpretations and traditions surrounding the Torah.
- **Shame / Kavod (כָּבוֹד)** – Kavod means "glory" or "weight," and in Hebraic thought, personal dignity was considered a reflection of one's relationship with God and community.

3. RECAP & REFLECTION (BOOK + DEVOTIONAL HIGHLIGHTS)

Book Recap – Dustprints of the Rabbi (Chapter 4):
Jesus lived and taught in a culture where honor was everything. But rather than pursue social prestige, He identified
with the shamed — and bore their disgrace. He didn't avoid
shame — He walked through it to redeem it. His cross
became the ultimate reversal of the honor-shame system.

Devotional Tie-In – Walking in the Dust (Week 4):
The devotional guided readers through stories of shame and
restoration — the woman at Jesus' feet, the Psalmist's cry,
and personal moments of being seen, even in weakness. It
challenged readers to let Jesus touch the places they still hide
— and to extend that restoration to others.

4. GROUP DISCUSSION QUESTIONS

Choose those that best fit your group size and spiritual
readiness:

1. *How did you see honor and shame functioning in this
   week's chapter or devotional?*
2. *What experiences have shaped how you view your own
   worth — especially in spiritual or church settings?*
3. *What part of your story do you find hardest to let Jesus
   touch or speak into?*
4. *How does the cross redefine what "being honored" means
   in God's Kingdom?*
5. *In what ways have you witnessed Jesus restore dignity
   — in your life or someone else's?*

5. DUSTPRINT DISCIPLESHIP CHALLENGE

Challenge Prompt (from Devotional):
Let Jesus reverse shame in you — and then help restore honor in someone else.

Invite your group to consider:

- Writing a letter of grace to someone who feels forgotten.
- Praying intentionally through past wounds and asking Jesus to speak truth.
- Taking a risk to speak publicly (in a safe space) about something once hidden.

6. CLOSING PRAYER & GROUP BLESSING

Prayer Prompt:
Jesus, You walked through shame so we could be clothed in Your honor. Touch what we still hide. Speak dignity into our silence. Teach us to see others with the same compassion You've shown us. Amen.

Optional Group Blessing (spoken together):

"We walk in the dust of the Rabbi — clothed not in shame, but in His honor."

SESSION 5 – SITTING AT HIS FEET

ALIGNED WITH CHAPTER 5 OF DUSTPRINTS OF THE RABBI & WEEK 5 OF WALKING IN THE DUST

Focus Verse

"Mary...sat at the Lord's feet listening to what He said."

— LUKE 10:39

Theme: Discipleship is not rooted in performance, but in presence. To sit at the Rabbi's feet is to adopt the posture of a *talmid* — choosing formation through stillness, attention, and nearness.

Leader Objective: By the end of this session, group members will understand the significance of "sitting at a rabbi's feet" in the Hebraic world, evaluate their own discipleship pace, and reflect on what needs to be surrendered in order to rest in Jesus' presence.

1. OPENING PRAYER & SHEMA

Prayer Prompt:
Jesus, we are so often in motion — and we confuse that with maturity. Slow us down. Center us in Your presence. Teach us to sit, to listen, and to be changed.
Amen.

Optional Shema (Deuteronomy 6:4–5):
"Hear, O Israel: The LORD our God, the LORD is one.
Love the LORD your God with all your heart and with all your soul and with all your strength."

---

2. GROUNDING IN THE DUST (CULTURAL INSIGHT)

In the time of Jesus, **to sit at a rabbi's feet** was an official posture of discipleship. It indicated a deep hunger for the rabbi's words and an eagerness to conform one's life to his interpretation of **Torah** — the divine teaching.

Torah (תּוֹרָה): *God's instruction. In the narrow sense, the first five books of the Hebrew Scriptures (Genesis–Deuteronomy), and in the broader sense, all of God's covenant teaching — both written and lived.*

Mishnah Insight:

"Let your house be a meeting place for sages; sit in the dust of their feet and drink in their words with thirst."

— AVOT 1:4

Mary of Bethany was doing something culturally radical by sitting at Jesus' feet. Not only was she behaving like a disciple — she was crossing cultural expectations for women in public learning spaces. Jesus honored this bold move, saying she had "chosen the better part."

Hebraic Terms Introduced This Week:

- **Torah** – The foundational teaching of Scripture, both written and lived.
- **Sitting at His Feet** – A formal disciple posture of submission, attentiveness, and hunger for a rabbi's halakhah.
- **Devekut (דְּבֵקוּת)** – "Clinging" or deep spiritual attachment to God or one's teacher.

3. RECAP & REFLECTION (BOOK + DEVOTIONAL HIGHLIGHTS)

Book Recap – Dustprints of the Rabbi (Chapter 5):
Jesus praises Mary for her posture, not her productivity. Her willingness to sit, stay, and listen stands in contrast to Martha's distracted service. Both were near Jesus — only one was learning in His dust. This chapter invites disciples to

slow down and resist the urge to earn what presence freely offers.

Devotional Tie-In – Walking in the Dust (Week 5):
The devotional focused on what it means to stop striving and simply sit. From the story of Mary to the personal challenge of being still before God, each day reminded readers that transformation often begins in sacred stillness — not activity.

4. GROUP DISCUSSION QUESTIONS

Choose 4–6 based on your group's interest and spiritual depth:

1. *What does it mean to "sit at Jesus' feet" in practical terms today?*
2. *Why do you think Mary's posture was considered so significant in her time — and ours?*
3. *Where do you see "Martha tendencies" in your own walk with Jesus?*
4. *How do silence, stillness, or prayerful listening play a role in your discipleship?*
5. *What's the difference between consuming information and becoming like the Rabbi?*

5. DUSTPRINT DISCIPLESHIP CHALLENGE

Challenge Prompt (from Devotional):
This week, make intentional space to sit — spiritually and physically.

- Choose a chair, corner, or journal space where you "sit at His feet."
- Read only one verse — slowly. Let it form you, not just inform you.
- If possible, eliminate one "productive" task this week to make room for presence.

6. CLOSING PRAYER & GROUP BLESSING

Prayer Prompt:
Jesus, You don't need our hustle — You long for our hearts. Teach us to stop. Teach us to sit. And when the world says, "Do more," remind us that You said, "Mary chose what is better."
Amen.

Optional Group Blessing (spoken together):

"We sit in the dust of the Rabbi — and we are changed in His presence."

SESSION 6 – IMITATING THE TEACHER

ALIGNED WITH CHAPTER 6 OF DUSTPRINTS OF THE RABBI & WEEK 6 OF WALKING IN THE DUST

Focus Verse

"Everyone who is fully trained will be like their teacher."

— LUKE 6:40

Theme: Discipleship is not only about believing in the Rabbi — it is about becoming like Him. The goal of the talmid was imitation in every word, deed, and response.

Leader Objective: By the end of this session, group members will explore the rabbinic expectation of imitation, reflect on where their lives mirror (or distort) Jesus, and identify a specific area where the Rabbi is inviting transformation through practice.

1. OPENING PRAYER & SHEMA

Prayer Prompt:
Jesus, You are not just our Savior — You are our model. Teach us to live how You lived, to speak how You spoke, and to love how You loved.
Amen.

Optional Shema (Deuteronomy 6:4–5):
"Hear, O Israel: The LORD our God, the LORD is one.
Love the LORD your God with all your heart and with all your soul and with all your strength."

---

2. GROUNDING IN THE DUST (CULTURAL INSIGHT)

In the rabbinic world, the highest aim of a **talmid (תלמיד)** was not to know what the rabbi knew — but to become who the rabbi was. You didn't become a disciple by collecting information, but by **imitating** the halakhah (way of walking) of your teacher.

Mishnah Insight:
"Get yourself a teacher... and cling to him."

— AVOT 1:6

This principle of **clinging** is known in Jewish thought as **devekut (דְּבֵקוּת)** — the act of drawing so close to your rabbi or to God that your thoughts, behavior, and essence become one with theirs.

> **Devekut** – *Spiritual nearness; clinging to the Rabbi or to God in deep trust and imitation. It's not only closeness — it's **attachment that transforms**.*

Hebraic Terms Introduced This Week:

- **Devekut** – Clinging, attachment; a heart-level devotion that results in imitation.
- **Halakhah** – "The way one walks" — lived theology.
- **Talmid** – A disciple who follows not just the words but the way of their rabbi.

3. RECAP & REFLECTION (BOOK + DEVOTIONAL HIGHLIGHTS)

Book Recap – Dustprints of the Rabbi (Chapter 6):
The journey of a disciple is never passive. It is dynamic imitation. Jesus didn't say, "Believe in Me" — He said, "Follow Me," and then modeled a life of prayer, mercy, rest, confrontation, and love. He called His disciples not to be fans of His teaching — but living reflections of His life.

Devotional Tie-In – Walking in the Dust (Week 6):
This week challenged readers to examine where their habits and instincts align — or misalign — with Jesus. Each day highlighted areas of quiet obedience: forgiveness, humility, prayer, and service. It emphasized that true imitation is visible in ordinary decisions.

4. GROUP DISCUSSION QUESTIONS

Choose the questions that fit your group's depth and direction:

1. *What does imitation look like in discipleship? How is it different from admiration?*
2. *Who in your life has modeled Jesus in a way that you wanted to imitate?*
3. *Where in your own life do you see the Rabbi's fingerprints — and where is He still forming you?*
4. *What is one habit or pattern of Jesus you want to take more seriously this season?*
5. *How do you experience **devekut** — clinging to Jesus — in your daily routines?*

5. DUSTPRINT DISCIPLESHIP CHALLENGE

Challenge Prompt (from Devotional):
This week, live as a visible reflection of the Rabbi:

- Choose one of Jesus' actions (e.g. praying early, forgiving boldly, serving quietly) and imitate it daily.
- Ask: *"If someone watched me today, would they know who I follow?"*
- Try writing out a summary of Jesus' life in one sentence — then align your day to it.

6. CLOSING PRAYER & GROUP BLESSING

Prayer Prompt:
Rabbi Jesus, You walked in holiness, but You invited us to follow.
Train our steps. Shape our words. Let our lives be evidence that we
walk behind You — and that we carry Your dust.
Amen.

Optional Group Blessing (spoken together):

> *"We walk in the dust of the Rabbi — and we are being*
> *changed to look like Him."*

SESSION 7 – THE COST OF THE CALL

ALIGNED WITH CHAPTER 7 OF DUSTPRINTS OF THE RABBI & WEEK 7 OF WALKING IN THE DUST

Focus Verse

"Whoever wants to be My disciple must deny themselves and take up their cross daily and follow Me."

— LUKE 9:23

Theme: Jesus doesn't hide the cost of discipleship. His call invites us not into comfort, but into covenant — where surrender opens the door to resurrection.

Leader Objective: By the end of this session, participants will understand the covenantal weight of following a rabbi, reflect on what they've had to leave behind (or are still holding on to), and name one step of surrender they are being invited to take.

1. OPENING PRAYER & SHEMA

Prayer Prompt:
*Rabbi Jesus, You never promised ease — but You promised Yourself.
Teach us to count the cost and walk forward anyway. Give us grace
to surrender, and trust to follow.
Amen.*

Optional Shema (Deuteronomy 6:4–5):
*"Hear, O Israel: The LORD our God, the LORD is one.
Love the LORD your God with all your heart and with all
your soul and with all your strength."*

---

2. GROUNDING IN THE DUST (CULTURAL INSIGHT)

In the first century, accepting a rabbi's invitation to follow
meant abandoning everything else — career, home, family
expectations, and sometimes even social standing. This
wasn't emotional conversion. It was a **covenantal surrender**.

Brit (בְּרִית): *Covenant — a sacred, binding agreement
between God and His people, always sealed in sacrifice.
Following a rabbi meant stepping into a brit-like commitment of loyalty and obedience.*

In the Jewish mindset, discipleship was never a half-step.
It was an all-of-life, whole-being response. That's why Jesus
called His disciples to "take up their cross." This was not just
about dying — it was about **belonging** to something that
redefined every other loyalty.

Hebraic Terms Introduced This Week:

- **Brit** – Covenant; the sacred framework of belonging and responsibility between God and His people.
- **Devekut** (reminder) – Clinging; choosing intimacy even when it costs you everything.
- **Talmid** – A disciple whose "yes" is lived, not just spoken.

3. RECAP & REFLECTION (BOOK + DEVOTIONAL HIGHLIGHTS)

Book Recap – Dustprints of the Rabbi (Chapter 7):
The call to follow Jesus is glorious — but costly. It means leaving nets, names, comforts, and self. Every disciple in Scripture gave up something to follow Jesus. This chapter reminds us that the Kingdom is free — but it will cost us everything.

Devotional Tie-In – Walking in the Dust (Week 7):
The devotional led readers through hard but honest reflections: walking away from security, facing ridicule, staying when quitting feels easier. It challenged them to redefine success and embrace cross-carrying not as failure — but as formation.

4. Group Discussion Questions

Select based on the maturity and readiness of your group:

1. *What part of this week's book or devotional content stood out to you most — and why?*

2. *What's the hardest part about following Jesus right now — emotionally, relationally, or practically?*
3. *What have you given up (or felt invited to give up) since choosing to follow Jesus?*
4. *How do you see covenant (brit) shaping how you follow?*
5. *What part of your life might be competing with your devotion to the Rabbi?*

5. DUSTPRINT DISCIPLESHIP CHALLENGE

Challenge Prompt (from Devotional):
This week, name your next surrender — and act on it.

- Write down the area of your life where Jesus is inviting deeper surrender.
- Tell one person what you're choosing to lay down — and why.
- Read Luke 9:23 aloud daily as a personal recommitment.

6. CLOSING PRAYER & GROUP BLESSING

Prayer Prompt:
Jesus, We want to follow You — not halfway, but all the way. Give us courage to drop the nets. Grace to count the cost. And strength to carry what You've called us to carry.
Amen.

Optional Group Blessing (spoken together):

"We walk in the dust of the Rabbi — not because it's easy, but because He is worthy."

SESSION 8 – TRUSTING THE DUSTY PATH

ALIGNED WITH CHAPTER 8 OF DUSTPRINTS OF THE RABBI & WEEK 8 OF WALKING IN THE DUST

Focus Verse

"Blessed are those who have not seen and yet have believed."

— JOHN 20:29B

Theme: The path behind the Rabbi is sometimes dry, uncertain, and unclear. But faith is not about seeing the full map — it's about trusting the One who walks ahead in the dust.

Leader Objective: By the end of this session, participants will understand biblical trust as a relational, covenantal response to uncertainty, reflect on their personal seasons of spiritual silence or wilderness, and name a specific step of trust they feel called to take now.

1. OPENING PRAYER & SHEMA

Prayer Prompt:
Rabbi Jesus, We don't always know where You are going. But we want to follow anyway. Help us trust when we cannot see — and teach us to walk even when the path disappears into the dust. Amen.

Optional Shema (Deuteronomy 6:4–5):
> *"Hear, O Israel: The LORD our God, the LORD is one.*
> *Love the LORD your God with all your heart and with all your soul and with all your strength."*

---

2. GROUNDING IN THE DUST (CULTURAL INSIGHT)

Faith in Hebrew is not primarily intellectual — it is **relational loyalty**. The Hebrew word for faith is **emunah (אֱמוּנָה)**, which means steadfastness, reliability, and deep trust. It is the posture of a disciple who keeps walking behind the Rabbi even when the road grows dim.

Emunah – *Trust, faith, loyalty; a lived commitment to God even when the outcome is uncertain. It is relational and covenantal, not merely doctrinal.*

Midbar (מִדְבָּר): *Wilderness — often a place of dryness and silence, but also the setting where God speaks (from davar, "word"). In Scripture, the wilderness is where faith is formed*

Midrash Insight:

"The desert is where the soul learns to listen."

— MIDRASH TEHILLIM 91

Jesus doesn't eliminate uncertainty — He walks with us through it. He doesn't give us all the answers, but He never leaves us alone on the path.

Hebraic Terms Introduced This Week:

- **Emunah** – Faithful trust; loyal obedience to God's voice, even in mystery.
- **Midbar** – Wilderness; a dry, lonely place often connected with divine encounter.
- **Davar** – Word; reminding us that the wilderness can also be where God speaks.

3. RECAP & REFLECTION (BOOK + DEVOTIONAL HIGHLIGHTS)

Book Recap – Dustprints of the Rabbi (Chapter 8):
The dusty path of discipleship is not always marked by clarity. Jesus' followers experienced stretches of uncertainty, wilderness, and confusion — but He called them to trust His presence more than their understanding. This chapter reminds us that following often means walking forward without full vision.

Devotional Tie-In – Walking in the Dust (Week 8):
The devotional offered stories of desert faith — Abraham,

Thomas, the wilderness wanderers — and invited readers to move forward without all the answers. Each day emphasized that trust is not passive — it's a daily choice to walk behind the Rabbi.

4. GROUP DISCUSSION QUESTIONS

Choose 4–6 questions that fit your group's context:

1. *How do you respond when God feels distant, silent, or unclear?*
2. *What does "emunah" (trust/faith) look like in your current season?*
3. *When have you seen spiritual growth result from walking in uncertainty?*
4. *What does it mean to follow the Rabbi when you cannot see His feet?*
5. *What "false maps" or expectations are you being invited to lay down?*

5. DUSTPRINT DISCIPLESHIP CHALLENGE

Challenge Prompt (from Devotional):
This week, choose to walk by **emunah**, not control:

- Identify one area where you are grasping for clarity instead of leaning into trust.
- Fast from one habit of control — excessive planning, information seeking, etc.
- Begin a "wilderness prayer" practice: one honest, short prayer of surrender daily.

6. CLOSING PRAYER & GROUP BLESSING

Prayer Prompt:
Jesus, You are the Rabbi who walks in silence and storms. Even when we cannot see You, we trust that You are ahead of us. Teach us to follow You through dry places — and let faith rise from the dust.
Amen.

Optional Group Blessing (spoken together):

"We walk in the dust of the Rabbi — even when we cannot see the road."

SESSION 9 – FOLLOWING THROUGH THE WILDERNESS

ALIGNED WITH CHAPTER 9 OF DUSTPRINTS OF THE RABBI & WEEK 9 OF WALKING IN THE DUST

Focus Verse

"He humbled you, causing you to hunger and then feeding you with manna... to teach you that man does not live on bread alone but on every word that comes from the mouth of the LORD."

— DEUTERONOMY 8:3

Theme: The wilderness is not the absence of God — it's the place where we learn to depend on His voice alone. Every disciple must follow through dry seasons, not around them.

Leader Objective: By the end of this session, participants will recognize the purpose of the wilderness in their spiritual formation, reflect on how God speaks in places of silence and struggle, and identify one practical way they can live out deeper dependence this week.

1. OPENING PRAYER & SHEMA

Prayer Prompt:
Jesus, You do not lead us into the wilderness to abandon us. You lead us there to speak, to shape, and to restore. Give us ears to hear Your voice — even in the silence.
Amen.

Optional Shema (Deuteronomy 6:4–5):
"Hear, O Israel: The LORD our God, the LORD is one.
Love the LORD your God with all your heart and with all your soul and with all your strength."

---

2. GROUNDING IN THE DUST (CULTURAL INSIGHT)

The Hebrew word for **wilderness** is **midbar** (מִדְבָּר) — but it shares its root with the word **davar** (דָּבָר), meaning "word" or "spoken thing." In the biblical mindset, the wilderness was not a place of silence — it was a place where God's voice became clear.

Midbar – *Wilderness; a dry, stripped place, but also the setting where divine revelation is received.*

Davar – *Word; what God speaks, often heard most clearly when other distractions are removed.*

The wilderness in Scripture is never accidental:

- Israel was formed in the wilderness.
- Jesus was tested in the wilderness.
- Prophets received vision in the wilderness.

Teshuvah (תְּשׁוּבָה): *Repentance or return. It means more than feeling sorry — it means realignment. In the wilderness, we are invited to return (shuv) to God's ways.*

Hebraic Terms Introduced This Week:

- **Midbar** – Wilderness; the environment of spiritual stripping, but also sacred encounter.
- **Davar** – Word; God's voice, often received most clearly in solitude.
- **Teshuvah** – Repentance; not just apology, but a return to trust and covenant faithfulness.

3. RECAP & REFLECTION (BOOK + DEVOTIONAL HIGHLIGHTS)

Book Recap – Dustprints of the Rabbi (Chapter 9):
The wilderness is not punishment — it's preparation. Jesus didn't bypass the desert; He walked into it. The chapter unpacks how the wilderness becomes the place where disciples unlearn false dependencies and learn to walk by God's daily provision and voice.

Devotional Tie-In – Walking in the Dust (Week 9):
This week helped readers see the desert as sacred space — a place of hunger, humility, provision, and formation. It also introduced the idea that while we often try to escape dry seasons, God may be using them to deepen our trust.

4. Group Discussion Questions

Choose 4–6 depending on your group's needs:

1. *What does the word "wilderness" bring up for you emotionally or spiritually?*
2. *Have you ever experienced God's voice more clearly in a time of dryness or difficulty?*
3. *What does it mean to hear a davar — not just a verse, but a word that shapes your next step?*
4. *What do you think God wants to form in you during your current (or past) wilderness season?*
5. *Where might God be inviting you into teshuvah — a return to trust?*

5. DUSTPRINT DISCIPLESHIP CHALLENGE

Challenge Prompt (from Devotional):
Live as one who listens in the wilderness:

- Choose a 5–10 minute block each day to sit in silence and simply ask: *"Speak, Lord. I am listening."*
- Reflect on where you've tried to fix or avoid your wilderness — and where God may be waiting to meet you in it.
- Write down a one-sentence *davar* you believe God is speaking to you right now.

6. CLOSING PRAYER & GROUP BLESSING

Prayer Prompt:
God of the Wilderness, We will not rush through the dry season. We will stay and listen. Let our hunger become holiness. Let our silence become surrender. And let Your Word form us in the dust.
Amen.

Optional Group Blessing (spoken together):

"We walk in the dust of the Rabbi — even in the wilderness, we follow His voice."

SESSION 10 – THE JOURNEY TO JERUSALEM

ALIGNED WITH CHAPTER 10 OF DUSTPRINTS OF THE RABBI & WEEK 10 OF WALKING IN THE DUST

FOCUS VERSE

"As the time approached for Him to be taken up to heaven, Jesus resolutely set out for Jerusalem."

— LUKE 9:51 (NIV)

Theme: Following Jesus will always lead us to Jerusalem — the place of purpose, surrender, and obedience. The path may be costly, but it is sacred.

Leader Objective: By the end of this session, group members will reflect on what "Jerusalem" represents in their own discipleship, recognize the need for intentional obedience, and take one step toward spiritual courage and clarity.

1. OPENING PRAYER & SHEMA

Prayer Prompt:
Jesus, You set Your face toward Jerusalem. Give us the courage to follow — even when we're afraid. Help us walk with intention, obedience, and covenant hope.
Amen.

Optional Shema (Deuteronomy 6:4–5):
"Hear, O Israel: The LORD our God, the LORD is one.
Love the LORD your God with all your heart and with all your soul and with all your strength."

---

2. GROUNDING IN THE DUST (CULTURAL INSIGHT)

In Scripture, **Jerusalem** is not just a city — it is a symbol of **God's dwelling, covenant fulfillment**, and the place where sacrifice and glory meet.

When Jesus "set His face toward Jerusalem," He was making a deeply intentional decision to fulfill His calling — not for fame, but for faithfulness.

This echoes the Hebraic concept of **kavanah (כַּוָּנָה)** — spiritual focus, devotion, or intentionality of heart and action.

Kavanah – *Direction of the heart; intentional focus on God's will when taking action, praying, or making decisions.*

Midrash Insight:

"All deeds are measured not only by what is done, but by the heart behind it."

— MIDRASH RABBAH, VAYIKRA 2:1

In Jewish thought, obedience without *kavanah* can be hollow. But when heart and action unite — even through fear or suffering — it becomes worship.

Hebraic Terms Introduced This Week:

- **Kavanah** – Intentionality; spiritual attentiveness or deliberate devotion to God's will.
- **Jerusalem** – Symbol of surrender, glory, and the place where obedience meets calling.

3. RECAP & REFLECTION (BOOK + DEVOTIONAL HIGHLIGHTS)

Book Recap – Dustprints of the Rabbi (Chapter 10):
Jesus' journey to Jerusalem wasn't passive — it was decisive. He walked toward His calling even knowing it would lead to betrayal and the cross. The chapter reminded readers that following the Rabbi requires us to move not toward comfort, but toward **consecrated surrender**.

Devotional Tie-In – Walking in the Dust (Week 10):
Each day challenged readers to consider their own "Jerusalem" — the place where God is calling them to obedience, even if it's difficult. The devotional emphasized that

courage and calling are often companions — and that we are not alone when we walk in the Rabbi's footsteps.

4. GROUP DISCUSSION QUESTIONS

Use 4–6 of the following to guide your session:

1. *What does "Jerusalem" represent in your current season of discipleship?*
2. *How do you respond when obedience is uncomfortable or costly?*
3. *What area of your life needs more kavanah — more spiritual intention?*
4. *Have you ever experienced peace or clarity on the other side of a difficult obedience?*
5. *How do you personally "set your face" like Jesus did — what helps you walk forward?*

5. DUSTPRINT DISCIPLESHIP CHALLENGE

Challenge Prompt (from Devotional):
Walk with *kavanah* this week — deliberate intention to follow Jesus where He's leading.

- Identify one action or decision you've been delaying — and take one step.
- Write a one-sentence prayer of *kavanah* to remind you of your purpose each day.
- Share your "Jerusalem journey" with someone in your group or community for support.

6. CLOSING PRAYER & GROUP BLESSING

Prayer Prompt:
Rabbi Jesus, You walked toward the cross with courage, not conve-
nience. Teach us to walk toward our calling with the same trust.
Wherever You go — to suffering, to surrender, to glory —
we want to follow. Let our hearts be fixed. Let our feet move. Let
our dust fall behind You.
Amen.

Optional Group Blessing (spoken together):

"We walk in the dust of the Rabbi — and we set our faces
toward Jerusalem."

SESSION 11 – THE HIDDEN STRENGTH (MEEKNESS)

ALIGNED WITH CHAPTER 11 OF
DUSTPRINTS OF THE RABBI & WEEK 11 OF
WALKING IN THE DUST

Focus Verse

"Blessed are the meek, for they will inherit the earth."

— MATTHEW 5:5

Theme: Meekness is not weakness. In the Kingdom of God, power is displayed through surrender, and true strength is often hidden in gentleness.

Leader Objective: By the end of this session, group members will understand the biblical and rabbinic concept of meekness, reflect on how power is used or withheld in their lives, and identify one way to walk in gentleness as Jesus did.

1. OPENING PRAYER & SHEMA

Prayer Prompt:
Rabbi Jesus, You did not need to prove Your power — You showed it in how You loved, how You knelt, and how You endured. Teach us the strength of surrender. Form in us the humility that reflects You.
Amen.

Optional Shema (Deuteronomy 6:4–5):
"Hear, O Israel: The LORD our God, the LORD is one.
Love the LORD your God with all your heart and with all your soul and with all your strength."

---

2. GROUNDING IN THE DUST (CULTURAL INSIGHT)

In Jesus' time, meekness was not admired. Strength was about visibility, dominance, and public honor. But Jesus redefined greatness through gentleness, restraint, and quiet faithfulness.

Anavah (עֲנָוָה): *The Hebrew word for "meekness" or "humility." It means knowing your strength but choosing to yield it — especially for the sake of others and the glory of God.*

Moses was described as the most **anav (humble)** man in all the earth (Numbers 12:3), yet he confronted Pharaoh and led a nation. Meekness was not inaction — it was **strength under guidance**.

Talmud Insight:

"Where there is humility, there is greatness."

— SOTAH 5A

Jesus embodied *anavah* when He washed feet, when He stayed silent before Pilate, and when He chose the cross over self-defense. His strength wasn't in what He could do — but in what He chose not to do.

Hebraic Terms Introduced This Week:

- **Anavah** – Meekness or humility; strength that chooses restraint for the sake of love and covenant.
- **Anav** – A humble one; a person who reflects God's character through submission, not self-promotion.

3. RECAP & REFLECTION (BOOK + DEVOTIONAL HIGHLIGHTS)

Book Recap – Dustprints of the Rabbi (Chapter 11):
This chapter reframes meekness as Jesus lived it — not timidity, but covenant restraint. The strongest person is often the one who stays when others run, who listens instead of reacts, and who serves instead of demanding recognition. Meekness marks those who walk closest to the Rabbi.

Devotional Tie-In – Walking in the Dust (Week 11):
Each day called readers to examine how they use power — in conversation, leadership, parenting, and pain. The devotional invited readers to see meekness as not what we lack, but

what we surrender for God's sake. It ended with a reflection
on legacy — that those who carry the dust of the Rabbi
inherit what the world overlooks.

4. GROUP DISCUSSION QUESTIONS

Select 4–6 for your setting:

1. *How would you define meekness before and after this
   week?*
2. *Where in your life is God inviting you to yield rather
   than react?*
3. *How do you see anavah reflected in Jesus' interactions
   with people?*
4. *When is gentleness more powerful than control?*
5. *What does it mean for the meek to "inherit the earth" in
   today's world?*

5. DUSTPRINT DISCIPLESHIP CHALLENGE

Challenge Prompt (from Devotional):
Practice *anavah* — quiet strength — in visible ways this week.

- Respond with gentleness in a conversation where
  you would normally press.
- Choose service over visibility — do something
  meaningful no one will see.
- Pray for the person you want to correct — and
  trust the Spirit to do the forming.

6. CLOSING PRAYER & GROUP BLESSING

Prayer Prompt:
Jesus, You bore the cross not because You had to — but because You chose to. Let that same strength live in us. When the world demands noise, make us quiet. When power tempts us, remind us of the towel. Form meekness in us — until we walk so closely behind You that Your dust softens our steps.
Amen.

Optional Group Blessing (spoken together):

"We walk in the dust of the Rabbi — with the quiet strength of meekness."

SESSION 12 – RABBI OF THE CROSS

ALIGNED WITH CHAPTER 12 OF
DUSTPRINTS OF THE RABBI & WEEK 12 OF
WALKING IN THE DUST

FOCUS VERSE

"Whoever wants to be My disciple must deny themselves and take up their cross and follow Me."

— LUKE 9:23

Theme: The Rabbi we follow walks to the cross — and calls us to carry ours. The cross is not just salvation — it is the shape of covenant obedience, sacrificial love, and resurrection hope.

Leader Objective: By the end of this session, group members will understand the significance of the cross in first-century Jewish context, reflect on what it means to carry their own, and name an area of discipleship where sacrifice and surrender are being invited.

1. OPENING PRAYER & SHEMA

Prayer Prompt:
Rabbi Jesus, You did not just teach us the way — You walked it, to the end. As we follow You to the cross, give us courage to carry what You place in our hands. Let surrender become our strength. Amen.

Optional Shema (Deuteronomy 6:4–5):
"Hear, O Israel: The LORD our God, the LORD is one.
Love the LORD your God with all your heart and with all your soul and with all your strength."

---

2. GROUNDING IN THE DUST (CULTURAL INSIGHT)

In the Roman world, the cross was a tool of shame, terror, and execution — especially for political rebels. To speak of carrying one was not poetic — it was shocking.

But Jesus redefined the cross as the mark of covenant love.

In Jewish tradition, **sacrifice** (*korban*, קָרְבָּן) was never senseless suffering. It was a means of drawing near to God. The Hebrew root *karav* (קָרַב) means **"to come close."**

Korban (קָרְבָּן)**:** *Sacrifice; that which brings one near to God.*

Midrash Insight:

"When one offers themselves in love, the fire of heaven draws near."

— MIDRASH TANCHUMA, TZAV 1

Jesus, as Rabbi and Messiah, carried the ultimate *korban* — offering not just His teaching, but His body, as the means by which His talmidim could walk the same path of self-giving love.

Hebraic Terms Introduced This Week:

- **Korban** – Sacrifice; an offering that brings one close to God, not simply an act of loss.
- **Karav** – To draw near; the root of the idea that sacrifice is not about death, but about nearness.

3. RECAP & REFLECTION (BOOK + DEVOTIONAL HIGHLIGHTS)

Book Recap – Dustprints of the Rabbi (Chapter 12):
Jesus taught His disciples to follow Him with their feet — but at the cross, He showed them how to follow with their whole lives. This chapter revealed that discipleship isn't measured by inspiration, but by the willingness to lay down our rights, our reputation, and even our safety to love as Jesus loved.

Devotional Tie-In – Walking in the Dust (Week 12):
Each day this week centered around the weight of the cross: the call to forgive, to endure, to remain silent in surrender.

Readers were invited not just to admire the cross — but to imitate it.

4. GROUP DISCUSSION QUESTIONS

Choose the questions that best fit your group's pace and depth:

1. *What stood out to you most about the cross this week — from the book or devotional?*
2. *What does it mean to "take up your cross" in practical, daily discipleship?*
3. *Where in your life is Jesus calling you to carry something hard, but holy?*
4. *How does understanding korban (sacrifice as drawing near) reframe the way you view surrender?*
5. *What keeps you from following the Rabbi into costly places — and what helps you stay close?*

5. DUSTPRINT DISCIPLESHIP CHALLENGE

Challenge Prompt (from Devotional):
This week, walk toward — not away from — your cross.

- Name the area of obedience that feels heavy but holy.
- Write out a prayer of surrender: "If this is my cross, I will carry it with You."
- Perform one quiet act of self-denial, not to prove something — but to draw closer to the Rabbi.

6. CLOSING PRAYER & GROUP BLESSING

Prayer Prompt:
Jesus, You did not carry the cross alone — and we don't have to either. You walk with us through surrender. You lead us through silence. You meet us in sacrifice. Help us to follow You — even here. Let the dust of Your cross fall on our feet.
Amen.

Optional Group Blessing (spoken together):

"We walk in the dust of the Rabbi — and we carry His cross in covenant love."

SESSION 13 – BEARING THE RABBI'S AUTHORITY

ALIGNED WITH CHAPTER 13 OF DUSTPRINTS OF THE RABBI & WEEK 13 OF WALKING IN THE DUST

FOCUS VERSE

"All authority in heaven and on earth has been given to Me. Therefore go and make disciples..."

— MATTHEW 28:18–19A

Theme: Discipleship doesn't end in following — it culminates in commissioning. Jesus shares His authority with those who walk in His dust so they can lead others into His way.

Leader Objective: By the end of this session, participants will understand how rabbinic authority functioned in the time of Jesus, reflect on their own responsibility to carry His name and teaching, and commit to represent Him faithfully in action and character.

1. OPENING PRAYER & SHEMA

Prayer Prompt:
Jesus, You gave us not just Your teaching but Your authority. Not to dominate — but to serve. Not to control — but to carry Your name well. Teach us to walk in that responsibility with grace.
Amen.

Optional Shema (Deuteronomy 6:4–5):
"Hear, O Israel: The LORD our God, the LORD is one.
Love the LORD your God with all your heart and with all your soul and with all your strength."

---

2. GROUNDING IN THE DUST (CULTURAL INSIGHT)

In the first-century rabbinic world, a rabbi could only commission disciples if he had **s'mikhah (סְמִיכָה)** — recognized authority to interpret Torah and pass it on. Most rabbis passed on traditions from earlier teachers. But Jesus taught with unprecedented authority — and then extended that authority to His disciples.

S'mikhah (סְמִיכָה): *The laying on of hands; the formal commissioning of a disciple to teach, judge, and act in the name of the one who sent them.*

When Jesus said, "As the Father has sent Me, I am sending you" (John 20:21), He wasn't giving the disciples a job — He was giving them His mantle. They were to become **living halakhah** — walking embodiments of His teaching.

Mishnah Insight:

"Be like the disciples of Aaron — loving peace and pursuing peace, loving people and bringing them close to Torah."

— AVOT 1:12

Authority in the Kingdom doesn't exalt. It lowers. It kneels. It carries towels, not titles.

Hebraic Terms Introduced This Week:

- **S'mikhah** – Rabbinic commissioning; the formal passing of authority from teacher to disciple.
- **Halakhah** – "Way of walking"; Jesus' authority is revealed in how His disciples walk.
- **Shaliach (שָׁלִיחַ)** – "One who is sent"; an agent or emissary acting in the name of another (root of the word apostle).

3. RECAP & REFLECTION (BOOK + DEVOTIONAL HIGHLIGHTS)

Book Recap – Dustprints of the Rabbi (Chapter 13):
Jesus didn't keep authority for Himself. He gave it to those covered in His dust — so they could teach what He taught, love whom He loved, and live how He lived. This chapter

explores how Jesus prepares His disciples not just to follow, but to *represent* Him.

Devotional Tie-In – Walking in the Dust (Week 13):
Each day challenged readers to consider how they carry the name of Jesus — in public and in private. Authority was framed not as power over people, but as responsibility before God. The devotional ended with the question: *Who will follow your dustprints — and will they find the Rabbi there?*

4. GROUP DISCUSSION QUESTIONS

Choose what suits your group:

1. What part of this week's chapter or devotional stood out most to you?
2. How does understanding *s'mikhah* and *shaliach* change the way you see the Great Commission?
3. In what ways are you carrying Jesus' name in your daily life?
4. Where do you feel confident in your calling — and where do you feel unqualified?
5. Who is following you, and what are your dustprints teaching them?

5. DUSTPRINT DISCIPLESHIP CHALLENGE

Challenge Prompt (from Devotional):
This week, walk with the intention of one who carries the Rabbi's authority:

- Speak boldly in love where you've been silent.

- Serve someone from a place of Kingdom representation — not convenience.
- Write down what it means to "be sent" — and ask God how to walk in that identity.

6. CLOSING PRAYER & GROUP BLESSING

Prayer Prompt:
Jesus, You have called us to walk in Your authority — not with pride, but with purpose. Not to be great, but to bring You near. Send us again — and let Your dust be on us as we go.
Amen.

Optional Group Blessing (spoken together):

"We walk in the dust of the Rabbi — and we carry His authority with humility."

SESSION 14 – A LEGACY OF DUSTPRINTS

ALIGNED WITH CHAPTER 14 OF DUSTPRINTS OF THE RABBI & WEEK 14 OF WALKING IN THE DUST

FOCUS VERSE

"Follow my example, as I follow the example of Christ."

— 1 CORINTHIANS 11:1

Theme: Discipleship doesn't end with belief — it continues through the lives we touch. Our dustprints were never meant to stop with us. They were meant to mark a path for others.

Leader Objective: By the end of this session, participants will reflect on the legacy of their own discipleship, recognize their influence on others, and commit to walking in a way that leads future disciples toward the Rabbi.

1. OPENING PRAYER & SHEMA

Prayer Prompt:
Rabbi Jesus, We followed You because You invited us to. Now, we want our lives to invite others too. Help us live in a way that points to You. Let our dustprints be faithful — and let them lead others Home.
Amen.

Optional Shema (Deuteronomy 6:4–5):
"Hear, O Israel: The LORD our God, the LORD is one.
Love the LORD your God with all your heart and with all your soul and with all your strength."

---

2. GROUNDING IN THE DUST (CULTURAL INSIGHT)

In Jewish tradition, legacy isn't measured by fame — but by **faithfulness**. A righteous person leaves behind something deeper than possessions — they leave a pattern, a path, and a trail that others can walk in.

Zechut (זְכוּת): *"Merit"; the enduring influence of one's righteous life on others. It often refers to the blessings that flow from the memory or actions of the faithful — sometimes generations later.*

Midrash Insight:
"The righteous leave behind not silver or gold, but deeds which shine like the firmament."

— MIDRASH TEHILLIM 112

Jesus didn't leave behind a building, an institution, or even a scroll of His own writing. He left behind **disciples**. That is His legacy — and ours.

Hebraic Terms Introduced This Week:

- **Zechut** – The merit or legacy of a faithful life; what endures and influences others long after we're gone.
- **Talmidim** – Disciples; our goal is not only to be formed, but to form others.

3. RECAP & REFLECTION (BOOK + DEVOTIONAL HIGHLIGHTS)

Book Recap – Dustprints of the Rabbi (Chapter 14):
This chapter reflects on how every step behind Jesus leaves a trail. The goal of discipleship isn't just to be changed — it's to live in a way that others can trace. From Peter to Paul to the Church today, our lives are part of the continuing story of the Rabbi's path.

Devotional Tie-In – Walking in the Dust (Week 14):
The devotional helped readers look back and look forward — to honor where they've walked, and to ask who might be

following them. The week closed with the challenge to live as one who walks in the dust and leaves a dustprint for the next generation.

4. GROUP DISCUSSION QUESTIONS

Choose 4–6 based on your group's reflection and engagement:

1. *What dustprints from others have helped form your walk with Jesus?*
2. *Who has been a faithful presence in your life, even when they didn't realize it?*
3. *What kind of legacy do you hope to leave behind — spiritually, relationally, practically?*
4. *What does zechut mean for how we live today, not just how we'll be remembered?*
5. *Who might be following your steps right now — and what are they seeing?*

5. DUSTPRINT DISCIPLESHIP CHALLENGE

Challenge Prompt (from Devotional):
This week, walk with legacy in mind:

- Write a letter, note, or prayer of blessing to someone younger in the faith.
- Share one story of your walk with Jesus with someone who needs it.
- Ask God to show you who is walking behind you — and how to guide them gently.

6. CLOSING PRAYER & GROUP BLESSING

Prayer Prompt:
Jesus, You invited us to follow You — and now, You call us to lead others. Not from expertise, but from our footsteps. Let the dust of our lives mark the path for the next generation. Let us walk faithfully, so others might find You in our trail.
Amen.

Optional Group Blessing (spoken together):

"We walk in the dust of the Rabbi — and we leave dustprints for others to follow."

EPILOGUE: STILL GUIDING IN THE DUST

YOU HAVE WALKED WITH YOUR GROUP FOR FOURTEEN WEEKS. You've opened the Word. You've asked the hard questions. You've listened, prayed, encouraged, and sometimes simply held the silence.

You didn't need to be perfect — just present. You didn't have to know it all — you just had to stay in the dust.

That's what leaders on the Covenant Path™ do. They walk a little ahead — not out of pride, but out of willingness. They go first in trust, first in humility, first in surrender. And by doing so, they make the path visible for others.

The truth is, leadership in the Kingdom of God is never about the spotlight. It's about the sandals. It's about carrying the dust of the Rabbi — and letting it fall behind you, so someone else can follow.

You've led faithfully. But this isn't the end. There will be more groups. More chapters. More wildernesses. More Jerusalem roads. More talmidim in need of a guide who knows how to walk, pause, and kneel.

So keep leading — in your home, your church, your workplace, your neighborhood. Keep guiding — not from authority, but from intimacy. Keep walking — not for admiration, but for impact. Because someone else is watching your dust. And the Rabbi is still walking ahead.

Final Blessing (Leader):

> *"May you continue to walk in the dust of the Rabbi.*
> *May your steps be steady.*
> *May your love be strong.*
> *May your life be legacy.*
> *And may those who walk behind you see not your*
>   *greatness —*
> *but the One who called you to follow."*

GLOSSARY OF HEBRAIC TERMS

A LEADER'S REFERENCE FOR THE COVENANT PATH™

Anav / Anavah (עָנָו / עֲנָוָה): Humility, Meekness – Strength under restraint; choosing gentleness, even when one has power. Seen in Moses and fulfilled in Jesus.

Brit (בְּרִית): Covenant – A sacred, binding agreement between God and His people. Always involves loyalty, sacrifice, and identity.

Davar (דָּבָר): Word / Thing Spoken – Refers to God's voice, often heard in the wilderness. Highlights the connection between revelation and location.

Devekut (דְּבֵקוּת): Clinging / Attachment – A deeply personal devotion to God or a rabbi, expressed through imitation and intimacy.

Emunah (אֱמוּנָה): Faith / Trust – Not just belief, but covenantal loyalty and trust expressed through faithful action, especially under uncertainty.

Halakhah (הֲלָכָה): The Way One Walks – A rabbi's interpretation and embodiment of Torah. A disciple imitates their rabbi's halakhah in daily life.

Karav / Korban (קָרַב / קָרְבָּן): To Draw Near / Sacrifice – A korban is a sacrifice offered to come close to God. Rooted in the idea that surrender leads to intimacy.

Kavanah (כַּוָּנָה): Intentionality – Direction of the heart in worship, obedience, or daily action. God desires not just the action, but the intention behind it.

Midbar (מִדְבָּר): Wilderness – A place of testing, silence, and encounter. Derived from the same root as *davar*, showing the wilderness as a place of revelation.

Midrash (מִדְרָשׁ): Interpretive Commentary – A rabbinic method of drawing out deeper meaning from Scripture through stories, questions, and creative engagement.

Mishnah (מִשְׁנָה): Oral Teaching – The foundational written record of Jewish oral law, compiled around 200 CE. Often cited in rabbinic thought alongside Torah.

Ol (עוֹל): Yoke – Symbol of rabbinic authority or teaching. Taking on a rabbi's *ol* means submitting to his interpretation and lifestyle.

Rabbi (רַבִּי): Teacher / Master – In the first century, a spiritual leader who taught and modeled how to live in covenant faithfulness to God.

S'mikhah (סְמִיכָה): Commissioning / Laying on of Hands –

A rabbi's authority to interpret Torah and commission disciples. Passed through generations by recognized lineage or divine endorsement.

Shaliach (שָׁלִיחַ): One Who Is Sent – An emissary or representative acting on behalf of another. Basis for the word *apostle* in Greek (apostolos).

Shema (שְׁמַע): "Hear" – The central Jewish prayer (Deuteronomy 6:4–5) declaring God's unity and calling for wholehearted love and obedience.

Tanakh (תַּנַ"ךְ): Hebrew Bible – Acronym for *Torah* (Law), *Nevi'im* (Prophets), and *Ketuvim* (Writings). The full Jewish canon of Scripture.

Talmid / Talmidim (תלמיד / תלמידים): Disciple(s) – One who follows a rabbi with the goal of becoming like him. Discipleship in this model is immersive, imitative, and covenantal.

Talmud (תַּלְמוּד): Rabbinic Commentary – A vast compilation of Mishnah and additional discussions (Gemara), preserving centuries of debate and interpretation.

Teshuvah (תְּשׁוּבָה): Return / Repentance – More than confession, it means turning around and realigning with God's covenant path.

Torah (תּוֹרָה): Instruction / Law – The core teaching of Scripture, traditionally the first five books of the Bible, but broadly refers to God's revealed way of life.

Zakar (זָכַר): Remember – To recall in a way that changes behavior. Covenant memory is active, not passive.

Zechut (זְכוּת): Merit / Legacy – The enduring spiritual impact of a righteous life, influencing generations beyond one's lifetime.